The Incredible
Kids' Craft-IT Series

Walter Foster

Print-n-Stamp
IT

Written and crafted
by Laura Stickney
Illustrated by Jeff Shelly

Print-n-Stamp It Contents

Walter Foster

The Incredible
Kids' Craft-IT Series

Print-n-Stamp IT

Written and crafted
by Laura Stickney
Illustrated by Jeff Shelly

Print-n-Stamp It Contents

Getting Started

Stamping and printing are all about surprises—when you peel off the paper from your stamp or printing plate to see what you've created, it's a magical moment. In this book, you'll use lots of "found" objects—like recycled odds and ends, bottle caps, string, yarn, paper tubes, sponges, and milk cartons—to stamp and print your own amazing designs. Each project you try and each print you make will be completely unique. And once you've tried stamping, you'll start to see all kinds of textures and possibilities everywhere around you!

Before you use any material or "found object" to stamp, check with a grownup to make sure it's okay to use. Go over the "Get It" list with a grownup before you start your Print-n-Stamp It craft so you can get some help gathering your materials. (Sometimes you may need an adult's help with a project, just to be safe.) In addition to your supplies and your grownup, find some old rags or newspapers to cover your workspace—your parents will appreciate it if you keep things clean.

Some supplies in the "Get It" list can be found around your home (such as white glue and scissors), but everything else is readily available at your local art and craft store. Check out the stamping and printmaking sections for stuff like water-based block printing ink and rubber rollers. And if an activity calls for a special pattern, look to the back of this book, where you'll find a tear-out section of all the patterns you'll need. If you want to make a pattern bigger or smaller to customize your project, ask an adult to help you duplicate it on a photocopier.

Enjoy finding new shapes to create crazy patterns and discovering other stuff to decorate with your printed designs. Most important, get creative and have fun!

Look for this symbol to let you know when a grownup's help is needed.

⚠ Watch It!
Look for this symbol to let you know when special care or precautions are needed.

Handy-Dandy Calendar

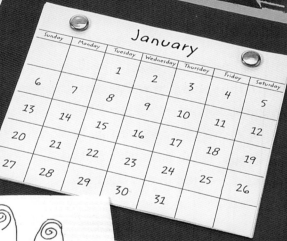

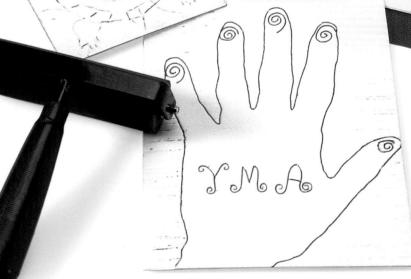

Don't stop at hand prints! You can trace everything from jelly jars to favorite toys—and then make the shapes into whatever you can dream up!

Get It!

Calendar pattern (page 33)
Water-soluble block printing inks
Smooth, nonporous printing surface
  (like a piece of lucite or Plexiglas™)
Pencil
Ballpoint pen
Foam plate or meat tray (clean)
Rubber rollers
Colored paper to print on
Poster board
Scissors
Hole punch
Glue stick
Ribbon
Brass fasteners (brads)

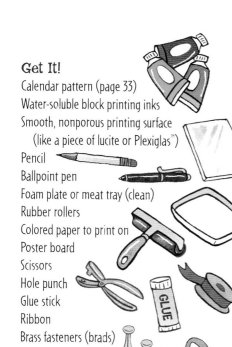

⚠ **Watch It!**

Ask a grownup for help when
punching holes through poster board.

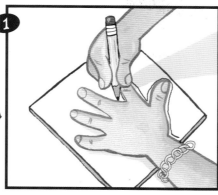

1 Cut a rectangle from a foam plate or meat tray. Cut off all the rims so that it's flat. Place your hand on the foam, and trace around it with a pencil, pressing a line into the foam as you go around.

2 Co over the drawing again with a ballpoint pen. Make the lines deep—but don't go through the foam! Then add some patterns to your design. To add a name or a word, write it backwards.

3 Choose 2 or 3 ink colors, and lay them side by side on your printing surface, making a stripe as wide as your roller. Roll over the ink in one direction several times. Then roll the ink onto your foam design, keeping the ink thin and even as you roll.

4 Lay the foam face down onto your colored paper. Carefully turn over the foam and paper (they'll be stuck together). Gently rub the back of the paper several times. Now peel the paper and foam apart, and allow the print to dry.

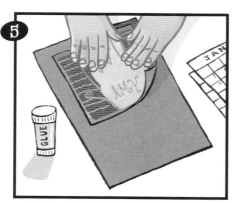

5 You may need to print your design several times to get a print you like. Then glue your print onto the poster board, and use the pattern to create the calendar pages.

6 Punch holes through the calendar pages, and poke holes through the poster board. Secure the calendar pages to the board with fasteners. Add a ribbon hanger at the top.

Totally Tubular Wrapping Paper

When you design your own wrapping paper, you're sure to be the hit of the party!

Choosing bright paint colors (or even metallics) to print your papers will make your presents stand out in a crowd!

Get It!

Toilet paper tubes, paper towel tubes, or other cardboard tubes

Scissors

Pencil

White glue

Glue brush

String, cords, or yarn

Tempera or poster paint

Paintbrushes

Papers to print on (such as brown or white butcher paper or thin colored paper)

Imagine It!

Try twisting or braiding pieces of yarn and string to get all sorts of fun and unique prints!

1 Cut a slit in one end of a tube, and insert one end of a long piece of string. Wrap the string tightly around the tube in a random pattern. When you get to the end, make another slit in the tube, and secure the end of the string.

3 Put some tempera paint (make sure it's not lumpy) into a dish. Brush paint over the string or yarn pattern on the tube, making sure to cover the entire pattern.

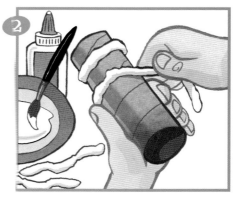

2 You can create a different pattern by brushing glue all over a tube and pressing pieces of yarn around it. Experiment with the spacing between the pieces of yarn as you glue them into place. Allow the tubes to dry overnight.

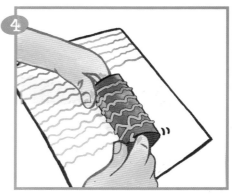

4 Hold the tube by the edges, and roll it all over your paper. Reapply color after each roll. Let your designs overlap, and see what cool patterns you can create!

Create some silly string stamps and give all your notes a personalized stamp of approval!

This stationery set makes a great gift—if you decide not to keep these super-cool notes to yourself!

Get It!

Thick cardboard

String or cord

Water-based block printing ink
   or tempera paint

Foam rollers

Smooth, nonporous printing surface
   (like a sheet of lucite or Plexiglas™)

White glue

Glue brush

Glue stick

Scissors

Colored cardstock—one piece
   13 ½" x 14 ' (34 cm x 35 cm), two
   pieces 1 ¾" x 4" (4.5 cm x 10 cm)

Assorted white envelopes, blank note
   cards, or blank writing paper

Ruler

1 Cut out small squares and rectangles from the thick cardboard. Brush glue onto the surface of one, and press a piece of string in a pattern into the wet glue. Get creative! Try squiggles, spirals, or wavy lines. Allow your stamps to dry overnight.

2 Squeeze out ink or pour some tempera onto the smooth printing surface. Roll the foam roller over the color several times until the roller is covered with paint. Now roll the color onto your stamp until it's completely covered.

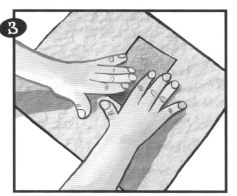

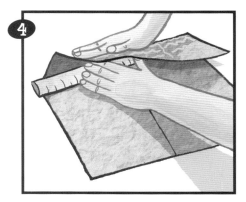

3 Press the stamp gently onto your cardstock. Re-apply color to your stamp and repeat. Use several stamps to create the paper, envelopes, and note cards. Try printing around the edges of the paper and onto the flaps of the envelopes.

4 Let everything dry overnight. For the folder, fold the heaviest piece of paper in half. Open it, and lay it face down. To create a pocket, measure 4" (10 cm) in from one of the tall edges, and fold the paper up against the edge of your ruler.

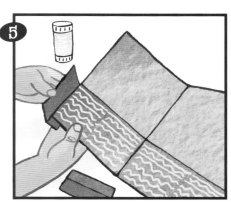

5 Rub the glue stick on the colored strips, and press the strips around the edges of the flap to seal the pockets. Fill the pockets with your printed stationery to complete the set!

Funky Book Covers

No one else will have book covers quite like these! Their funky techno style will make your books look unique— from cover to cover!

Finders keepers! Use plastic bottles, caps, lids, flower pot liners, grids, netting, or anything else you find that has a cool printing texture!

Get It!

Found objects
   (such as bottle caps or netting)
Shopping bags, butcher paper,
   or colored craft paper, large enough
   to cover your books
Acrylic paint
Foam roller
Foam plate
Books to cover

Gather some objects with obvious texture. Then pour some paint on a plate. Roll the foam roller in the paint, and then roll it over one of the objects for an overall background print.

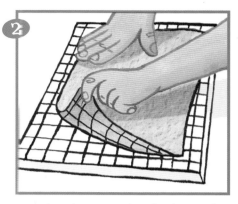

Lay a piece of paper over the painted, textured object, and rub the back of the paper with your hand to get an even print. Then slowly peel off the paper and set it aside.

Choose more objects, and repeat the process, using a different color for each texture. Re-roll your textured item with paint after each stamping.

Allow the paint to dry, and then lay the printed paper face down. Fold the paper against the bottom and top edges of the book and crease.

Fold along the creases, and wrap the ends of the paper around the covers of your book. Slip the covers into the paper pockets.

Magical Memory Album

Keep favorite pics and mementos in a totally hip place— your own unique album!

You can find photo corners in fun colors at an art and craft store in the scrapbook section. They'll keep your photos in place with style!

Get It!

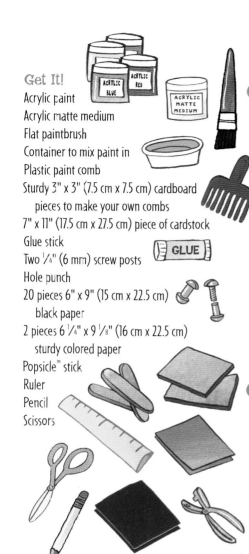

Acrylic paint

Acrylic matte medium

Flat paintbrush

Container to mix paint in

Plastic paint comb

Sturdy 3" x 3" (7.5 cm x 7.5 cm) cardboard
    pieces to make your own combs

7" x 11" (17.5 cm x 27.5 cm) piece of cardstock

Glue stick

Two ¼" (6 mm) screw posts

Hole punch

20 pieces 6" x 9" (15 cm x 22.5 cm)
    black paper

2 pieces 6 ¼" x 9 ⅛" (16 cm x 22.5 cm)
    sturdy colored paper

Popsicle™ stick

Ruler

Pencil

Scissors

1 Make your own comb by cutting some notches out of a small piece of thick cardboard. Make your comb look different (different-sized teeth or different spaces between the teeth) from the purchased plastic comb.

2 Next mix some paint with a little matte medium. Dip your brush into the mixture, and spread it quickly over the piece of cardstock, covering the entire sheet. Before the paint dries, run the plastic comb through it to make some wavy lines.

3 Use the other comb to pull through the wet paint in a different direction. Experiment with straight lines and wavy lines, and try using different colors. Allow the combed paper to dry completely.

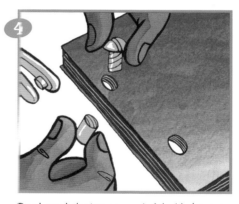

4 Punch two holes into one end of the black papers and the two colored paper covers. Make sure all the holes line up, and then use the screw posts (one at a time) to attach all the papers together.

5 Measure and mark 1" (2.5 cm) from the side of the album. Lay a ruler at this mark, and run a Popsicle stick against it to create a bend in the front cover.

6 Cut the dry combed paper to fit the cover. Glue it to the front, and let it dry completely. Now you can add pictures and other decorative stuff!

Fab Photo Frame Box

This box is the purr-fect place to stash your snapshots—you'll be able to track down your favorite photos anytime!

Feature a favorite pic in a prime spot on top of your box—then display it in your bedroom for everyone to admire!

Get It!

Box patterns (pages 35-37)
Acrylic paint
Containers for paint
Paintbrush
1 sheet soft foam
White glue
Small blocks of wood
Pencil
Scissors
1 large sheet colored poster board
Brass fasteners (brads)
Hole punch
Popsicle™ stick
Ruler
Mat for photo frame
Masking tape

⚠ Watch It!
Ask a grownup for help when punching holes through cardboard.

1 Use the pattern to trace and cut out the box and lid from a sheet of poster board. Bend the box as shown, using a Popsicle stick and a ruler to score the board.

2 Now fold and glue the tabs to create a box. For the lid, double fold one long side to create a reinforced edge for the lid hinge. Glue the corner tabs to the inside of the lid.

3 Punch three holes in the lid hinge. Place the lid on the box, and trace inside the holes onto the back of the box. Now punch holes in the box at those marks, and secure the lid with brads.

4 Use masking tape to create a hinge between the box and the mat. Place a picture in the frame. Ask an adult to help you punch a hole in the frame and the box. Secure with a brad.

5 To make stamps, draw some shapes on foam with a pencil, and cut them out. Glue them to wood blocks. Make as many different stamps as you want! Allow the glue to dry thoroughly.

6 Hold the side of the box with your hand, or fill it with books to make a good stamping surface. Brush paint onto a stamp, and press it onto your box (don't forget the sides and the corners too!).

Spongy Gift Bags

Make any gift extra special by stashing it in one of these colorfully printed bags!

You can use old kitchen sponges for your stamps; just make sure they're clean (and don't forget to ask a grownup if it's okay).

Get It!

Permanent marker
Sponges
Scissors
Poster paint
Paintbrush
Blank shopping bags with handles
Cardstock, smaller than a lunch bag
Hole punch
Ribbon
Brown lunch bags

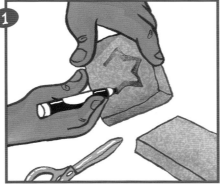

1. Draw some simple shapes onto dry sponges with a permanent marker, and cut them out. If a sponge is hard to cut, wet it slightly, and pinch the sponge as you cut.

2. Brush some paint onto a sponge shape. Stamp your shape onto one side of a blank bag. Now let the printed side of the bag dry completely before you print the second side.

Imagine It!

Who says you have to stick to shapes? You could also trace and cut out some sponge letters—then stamp out a name or a phrase (like "Happy Birthday!" or "Let's Celebrate!").

3. Create a gift tag by stamping onto a small piece of cardstock. Let it dry, and then fold the card in half. Punch a hole in the corner, and attach it to your gift bag handle with a ribbon.

4. You can also make a gift bag out of a sandwich bag by printing on a separate piece of cardstock and gluing it to the bag. Cut the edges with wavy scissors and add ribbon!

Stenciled Pop-Up Cards

There's a surprise inside of these cards—learn to use a stencil for picture-perfect pop-ups!

Go beyond butterflies! Ladybugs, leaves, and flowers all make great cards—naturally!

Get It!

Butterfly card patterns
(pages 38–39)
Manila file folders
Pencil
Poster or acrylic paint
Containers for paint
Paintbrushes
Small sponge pieces
Masking tape
Scissors
Two 7" x 10" (17.5 cm x 25 cm) sheets
colored cardstock
Glue stick
Paper doilies

Butterfly Card

1 Trace the butterfly pattern on the folded edge of a manila folder. Cut out the butterfly. Then trace and cut out a flower and a circle.

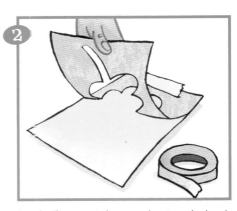

2 Lay the flower stencil on top of a piece of colored cardstock, and tape it in place at the edges. Apply some paint (not too much) to a sponge.

3 Pat the sponge gently over the flower stencil, letting the paper color show through a little. Then lay the circle stencil over your printed flower, and apply a second color for the flower's center.

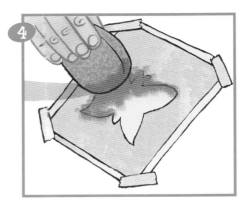

4 Lay the butterfly stencil over another piece of cardstock, and tape it down. Choose a bright color, and paint your butterfly. Then let everything dry before you move on to the next step.

Imagine It!

Instead of purchasing Valentines this year, make special pop-up heart cards for your friends, teachers, classmates, and family!

Butterfly Card continued on next page

Cut out the butterfly, leaving a small border around the outside. Use a sponge to dab on another bright color through a doily to create the design on the wings.

Use another piece of cardstock for the cover of the card. Lay the doily on the cover, and sponge on a design at the bottom. Let all of your prints dry completely.

Fold the flower print in half, with the image inside. Cut two 1" (2.5 cm) slits in the center of the card, about 1" (2.5 cm) apart, to create a tab (but don't cut through the center!).

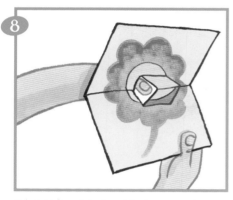

Now fold the tab back and forth to crease it even more. The tab is what will make your butterfly pop out of the card! Push the tab forward, and then fold the card in half again.

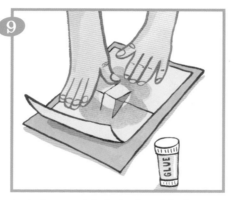

Apply glue around the back edges of the flower print, and glue it to the cover, starting at the top and working your way down. Smooth out the surface with your hands so there are no wrinkles.

Apply glue to the lower tip of the butterfly. Before you glue it to the tab, center the butterfly in the card, and make sure it can be smoothly opened and closed without any edges sticking out.

Get It!

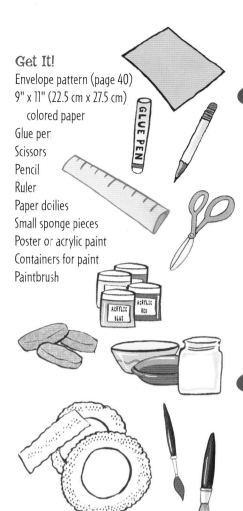

Envelope pattern (page 40)
9" x 11" (22.5 cm x 27.5 cm)
   colored paper
Glue pen
Scissors
Pencil
Ruler
Paper doilies
Small sponge pieces
Poster or acrylic paint
Containers for paint
Paintbrush

Envelopes

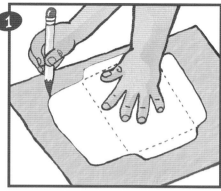

1 Trace the envelope pattern onto the back of the colored paper. Mark the dotted fold lines, and cut along the solid lines.

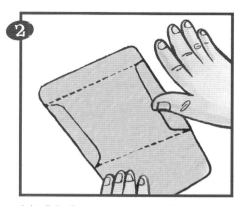

2 Fold all the flaps in toward the middle, and crease the folds with your thumbnail. Open up the top and bottom flaps.

3 Dab the sides of the bottom flap with the glue pen, and fold the flap up to meet the side flaps. Press firmly, and let dry.

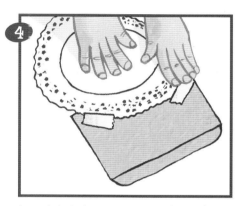

4 Lay a doily in place at one edge of the envelope. You may want to tape it in place so your paint doesn't smudge.

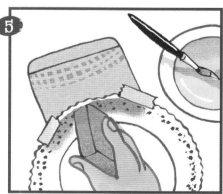

5 Load your sponge with paint, and gently dab it on the doily to print a lacy pattern on your envelope. Repeat around the other edges to complete your envelope design!

Naturally Wonderful Desk Set

Next time you're out on a nature walk, collect some leaves to create your own printed natural wonders!

Try experimenting with other objects you've found outdoors.

Get It!

Leaves, grasses, and sticks
Foam rollers
Acrylic paint
Foam plate
3 pieces of 19 1/2" x 25 1/2" (49 cm x 64 cm) colored paper
Scrap paper (or pieces of torn newspaper)

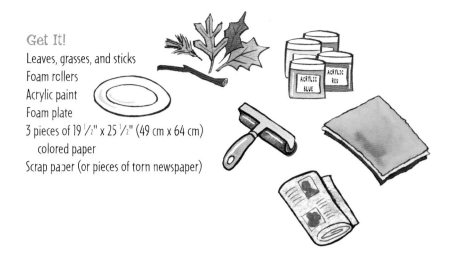

Printed Leaf Paper

Lay one sheet of large colored paper on your workspace, making sure there's nothing bumpy underneath it. Moisten your roller with paint, covering the roller evenly.

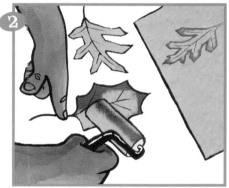

Apply several thin coats of paint to one side of a leaf with the roller. Gently press the painted side of the leaf down. Set a piece of clean scrap paper on top, and rub the back.

Repeat this process all over your paper. Try other leaves, sticks, and dry grasses to create interesting patterns. Then allow everything to dry.

Get It!

15" x 20" (37.5 cm x 50 cm) heavy cardboard with a smooth surface

Corrugated cardboard, at least 6" x 15" (15 cm x 37.5 cm)

Printed leaf papers

Glue stick

Scissors

Ruler

Pencil

White glue

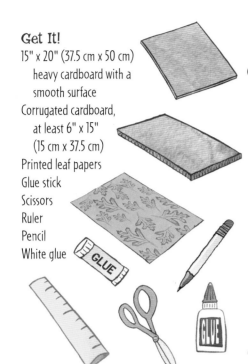

Watch It!

Ask a grownup for help when cutting the cardboard.

Blotter

1 Cut one of the printed papers to 17" x 22" (42.5 cm x 55 cm). Lay it face down on your workspace, and glue it to the heavy board, leaving an even border around the outside.

2 Cut off all four paper corners, leaving 1/8" (3 mm) between your cut and the corner of the heavy board. Now you'll have paper flaps to wrap around the board.

3 Apply glue to one of the flaps, and wrap it around the edge of the board. Repeat for the rest of the paper flaps, and then set the board aside to dry. If needed, put some books on top to flatten.

4 Have an adult help you cut two pieces of corrugated cardboard to 2 1/2" x 15" (6 cm x 37.5 cm) for the side flaps. Then cut two pieces of leaf paper to match, leaving at least one extra inch all around.

5 Wrap and glue the side flaps. Then glue them to the board using white glue, leaving the insides open so you'll be able to slide notes and papers into your blotter.

Get It!

Printed leaf paper
Clean, empty soup can
4 1/4" x 6 1/2" (11 cm x 16 cm) cardboard
3" x 5" (7.5 cm x 12.5 cm) note pad
Measuring tape
White glue
Glue brush
Scissors
Ruler
Pencil
Glue stick

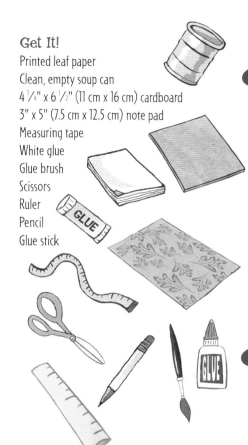

Pencil Cup

First make sure the can is clean and dry. Measure its height, and then measure around the outside too. Mark the measurements lightly with pencil on your leaf paper.

Cut the paper for the can. Make sure to leave an extra 1" (2.5 cm) on the side edges so you'll be able to overlap the paper when you wrap it around the can.

Brush glue on the can at the seams and along the rims. Wrap the printed paper around it, smoothing it out as you go. Hold it in place until the glue sets, and then let it dry completely.

Memo Pad

Cut the leaf paper to 6 1/4" x 8 1/4" (16 cm x 21 cm), and wrap and glue it around the cardboard the same way you did with the blotter. Press out any wrinkles with your hands.

Cut another piece of paper into a 2" x 10" (5 cm x 25 cm) strip. Then measure 3/4" (2 cm) down from the top of your board, and mark the spot lightly with a pencil. This is your guideline for step 3.

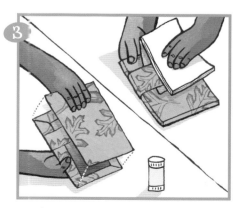

Fold the strip around the board at your marked line, and use a glue stick to attach it to the back of the board. Cover the back with more leaf paper, and insert your note pad under the strip.

Veggie Print Apron

Instead of eating your veggies, use them to print your own design!

Experiment with other fruits and vegetables to see what kind of stamps they make—mushrooms, onions, and apples are all good ones to try.

Get It!

Cutting board
Table knife
Celery
Green bell pepper
Yellow squash
Cloth apron
Fabric paints
Paintbrushes
Containers for paint
Newspaper

1 Working on a cutting board (with a grownup's help), cut the vegetables evenly to create flat surfaces for printing. Slice off the end of the celery, and cut the squash and bell pepper in half lengthwise. Dry off all the cut vegetables thoroughly.

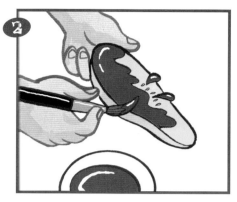

2 Cover your workspace with an extra padding of newspaper, and lay the apron flat on top. Brush fabric paint onto the cut surface of the squash, and press the whole thing down to print a butterfly's body evenly on your apron.

3 Now brush paint onto the pepper, and stamp in the wings. Apply more paint each time you stamp. Use the celery to create the antennae.

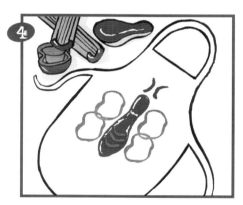

4 Once the body is dry, use another color on a second piece of celery. Stamp it over the body to create stripes. Allow your apron to dry completely.

⚠ Watch It!

- Ask a grownup for help when using a knife.
- Your fabric paint may require a heat setting—follow the directions on the bottle, and ask for a grownup's help.

27

Marvelous Muffin Tin Monoprint

Whether you keep this book all tied up or hang it on the wall, your printed pages will impress any cook!

Cherry Pie

Spaghetti Sauce

Noodle Soup

Vegetable Soup

olive oil, 1 onion chopped
stalks cubed
peeled and
ped spin

Pizza Dough

Write your favorite recipes neatly on index cards to match your recipe book. Include some family favorites to make it a colorful keepsake!

Get It!

Cherry pattern (page 38)
Small metal muffin tin
    (washed to remove
    any grease)
Poster paint
Paintbrushes
Containers for paint and water
3 pieces of 6 ¼" x 7 ½" (16 cm x 19 cm)
    colored paper
Glue stick
Scissors
Popsicle™ stick
6" x 35" (15 cm x 87.5 cm) paper strip
2 pieces 5" x 6 ½" (12.5 cm x 16 cm) mat
    board or cardboard
Thin ribbon or cord
Hole punch
Eight 4" x 5 ¼" (10 cm x 13 cm) envelopes
Eight 3" x 5" (7.5 cm x 12.5 cm) index cards

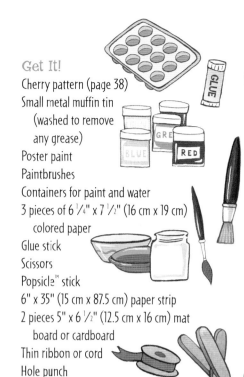

1

Paint the cherry design on the flat bottoms of your muffin tin. Work quickly so your paint doesn't dry out. Then lay a piece of colored paper onto the tin. Carefully press the back of the paper with your fingertips to transfer the design.

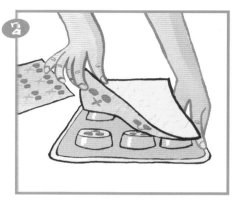

2

Gently peel the paper off the tin and set it aside to dry. You'll need to make at least three sheets. (Keep your favorites for the covers!) Each time you print, repaint your tin with the pattern. Then let everything dry.

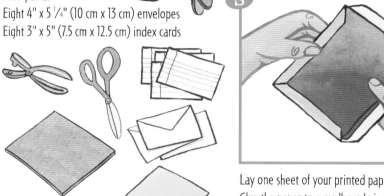

3

Lay one sheet of your printed paper face down. Glue the paper to a cardboard piece, leaving an edge around the board. Smooth it out, and then glue the other cover together. Now trim the corners, and glue the edges down. Let the covers dry.

4

Cut off the top flaps of your envelopes. Cut out some cherry circles from your extra prints, and glue them to your envelopes. Fold the long strip of paper in half, and then fold it in half twice more, creasing each fold with a Popsicle stick.

5

Open up the strip, and refold as shown (accordion style). Glue the top and bottom panels of the paper to the covers, centering them carefully.

6

Now glue the envelopes onto the paper as shown. Punch a hole in the top cover, and attach a ribbon. Fill the envelopes with your favorite recipes!

Milk Carton Treasure Box

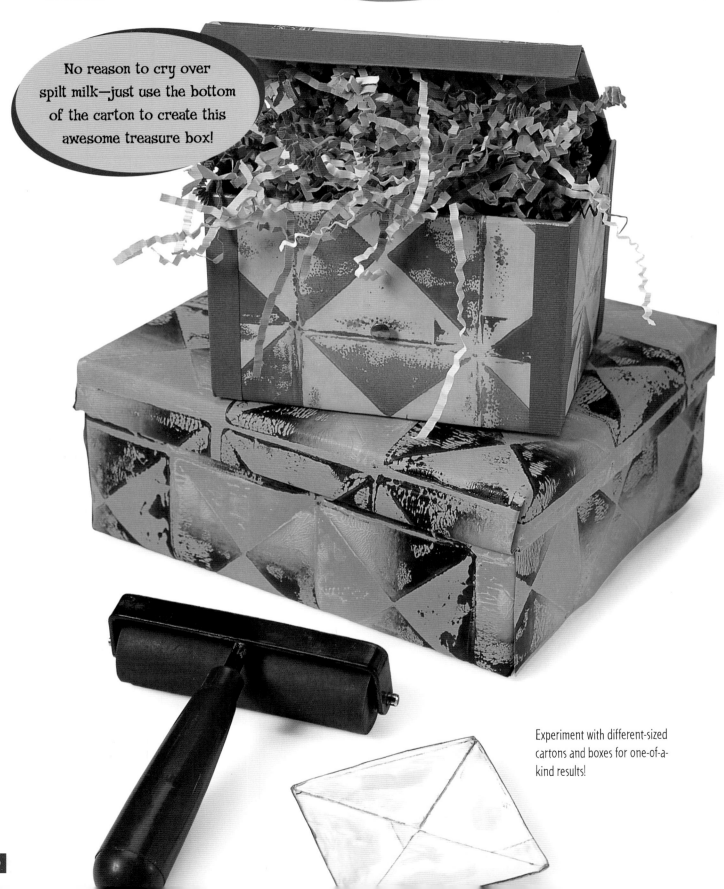

No reason to cry over spilt milk—just use the bottom of the carton to create this awesome treasure box!

Experiment with different-sized cartons and boxes for one-of-a-kind results!

Get It!

Water-based block printing ink
Rubber roller
Smooth, nonporous printing
   surface (like Plexiglas™)
Milk carton
Scissors
Small shoebox with lid
Butcher paper or colored craft paper,
   big enough to cover the box
Glue stick
Ruler
Pencil

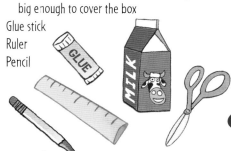

⚠ Watch It!
Ask a grownup for help
cutting the milk carton.

1 Have a grownup help you cut out the bottom of the milk carton. Then squeeze stripes of three ink colors out onto your printing surface.

2 Roll the roller back and forth to cover it evenly with ink, and then roll it over the milk carton piece (the side with the raised triangles).

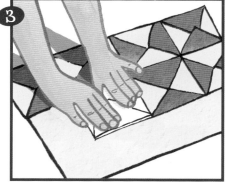

3 Place the inked piece face down onto your paper. Press down with your fingers, and rub the back. Re-ink the piece after each stamping. See what patterns you can create by turning your stamp in different directions.

4 Allow the paper to dry completely. Then lay the paper face down, and trace around the outside of the box and the lid, leaving at least 1" (2.5 cm) extra around each side of both pieces. These will become the flaps that wrap around the box.

5 Cut out the paper to wrap your box and lid, using the outermost line you traced as a guideline. Then fold the paper along the guidelines to crease it.

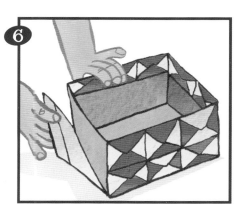

6 Wrap your box and lid with the printed paper, and glue it down. If you like, finish off the corners with colored paper strips.

Follow-It Project Patterns

This is where you'll find a special tear-out section of all the patterns you'll need. If you want to make a pattern bigger or smaller to customize your project, ask a grownup to help you to enlarge or reduce it on a photocopier.

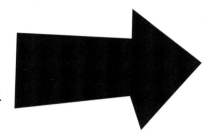

Walter Foster®

Walter Foster Publishing, Inc.
23062 La Cadena Drive
Laguna Hills, California 92653
www.walterfoster.com
© 2002 Walter Foster Publishing, Inc.
All rights reserved.

The author wishes to thank Vilma Mendillo for her time and assistance.
Special thanks to Stephanie Sarracino and the students at Bonita Canyon Elementary School
and to Robyn Allen and the students at Huntington Seacliff Elementary School for their contributions as craft consultants.

Order Code: IT05
ISBN: 1-56010-651-4
UPC: 0-50283-86405-9

Produced by the creative team at Walter Foster Publishing, Inc.:
Sydney Sprague, Associate Publisher
Pauline Foster, Art Director/Designer
Barbara Kimmel, Senior Editor
Samantha Chagollan and Jenna Winterberg, Editors
Carole Thorpe, Production Designer
Toni Gardner, Production Manager
Kathy Beeler, Production Coordinator
Monica Noemi Mijares-DeCuir, Production Artist

Printed in Korea.

Calendar Pattern (Page 5)

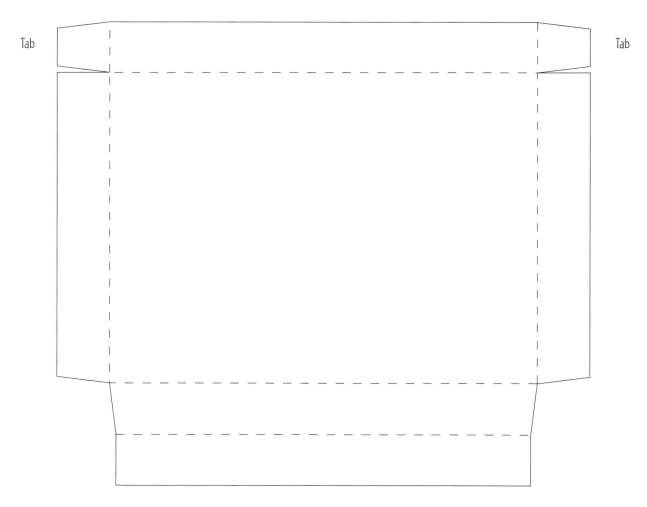

Tab

Tab

Lid Hinge

Photo Frame Box Pattern (Page 15)

To make the box, first photocopy the pattern. Then overlap the crosshairs (–⊕–) from the two separate pages. Tape the pattern where the two pages meet, and cut it out. Then follow the directions on page 15.

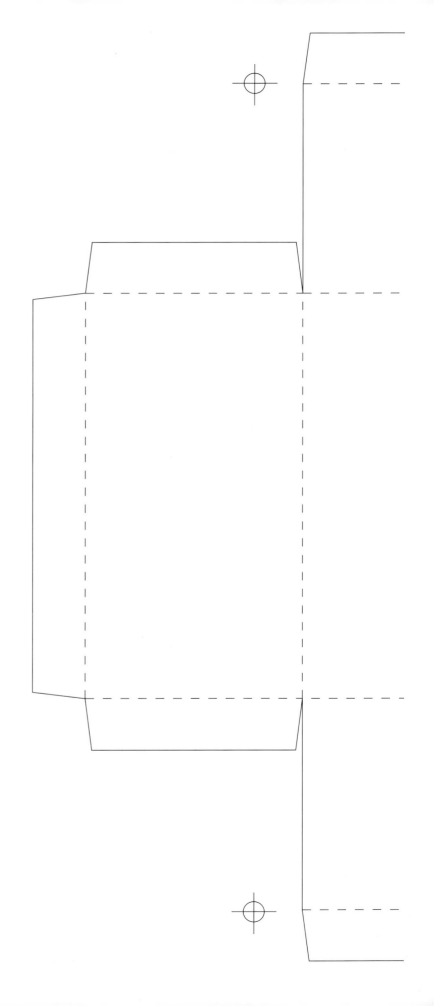

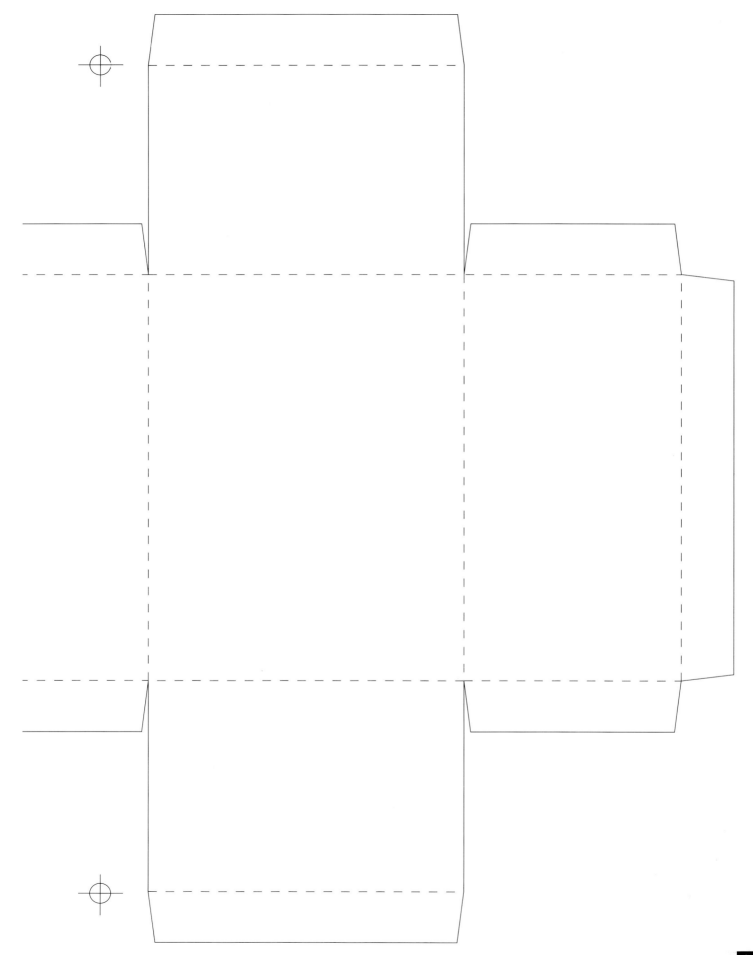

37

Pop-Up Butterfly Card Pattern (Page 19)

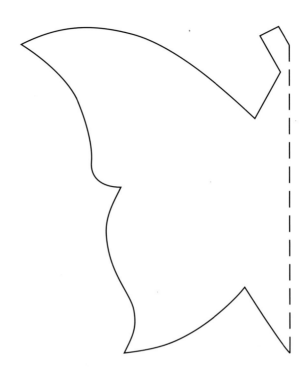

Muffin Tin Cherry Pattern (Page 29)

Make two copies of this pattern. Cut all the way around the outline of the flower on one copy; this will be your flower stencil. On the second copy, cut out only the center hole. This will be your circle stencil.

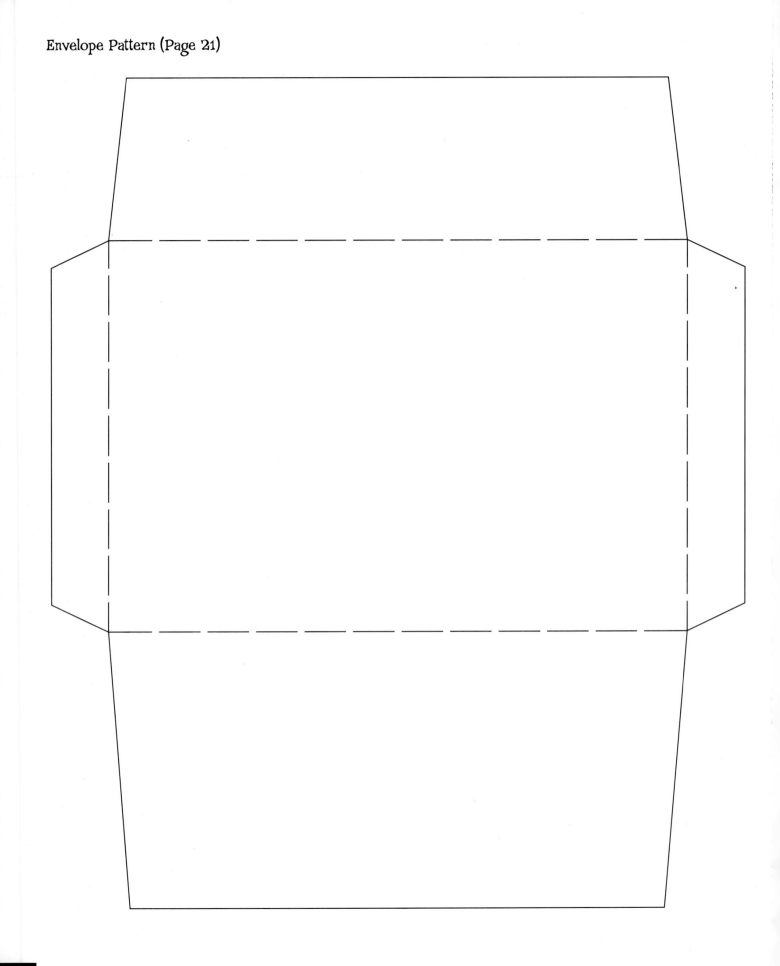